Ceremonial rattles with beadwork and painted gourds. Made by Rosita Bitsuie. Courtesy, Arroyo Trading Post.

Contents

Navajo doll representing a kachina dancer. Courtesy, Private Collection.

Navajo clay figures representing the Yei bi chei dancers, 1987. Courtesy Adobe Gallery.

WEAVING

Geometric, Pictorial and Miniature

The nomadic Navajo people may have witnessed weaving first when they encountered the Pueblo groups along the Rio Grande River in northern New Mexico several centuries ago. By the time Spanish explorers introduced sheep in the sixteenth century and recorded the first written accounts of the region, the Navajo were weaving native-grown cotton. Lightweight wearing blankets were made up to the early twentieth century when traders encouraged the weaving of heavier materials for rugs. Saddle blankets of striped design continue to be made as they have throughout the decades. Today, many weavings are hung on walls as fine tapestries.

Geometric patterns in natural colors and vegetal and commercially dyed colors can be generally grouped by regional styles. Also, imaginative figurative designs known as "pictorials," which can be seen as Navajo folk art, and miniature weavings, have developed primarily for sale to visitors of the Southwest region.

Two-faced saddle blanket, Wide Ruins style on one side and stripes on the reverse. Courtesy, Private Collection.

Navajo Arts and Crafts

Nancy N. Schiffer

Schiffer Publishing Ltd

1469 Morstein Road, West Chester, Pennsylvania 19380

Two weaving looms, these for miniature rugs, demonstrating the traditional Navajo upright style. Courtesy, Private Collection.

Front cover:
Weaving. Woven by Ruth Harvey. Courtesy, Private Collection.

Morning Dance doll, wood, leather, feathers, moss, beads. Made by Leslie Francisco. 13″ x 3″ x 3″. Courtesy, Shiprock Trading Company.

Hawk fetish, serpentine. Courtesy, Palms Trading Company.

Pottery, three small handleless pots. Made by S.W. 3½″, 3½″, 4″. Courtesy, Shiprock Trading Company.

Basket. 3″ x 11″. Courtesy, Foutz Trading Company.

Back cover:
"Wolf dancer". Made by Tim Washburn. 18″ x 6″ x 6″. Courtesy, Arroyo Trading Post.

Sandpainting with relief shield and fetish bear. Made by Jerald Sherman. 24″ x 18″. Courtesy, Arroyo Trading Post.

Turquoise jewelry. Made by Perry Shorty. Shown against a weaving by Brenda Spencer, Wide Ruins, AZ. 30″ x 42″. Courtesy, Hubbell Trading Post.

Painting. Painted by R. Chee. 12″ x 12″. Courtesy, Private Collection.

Photographs of landscapes on Navajo lands by H.L. James. Photographs of the objects by Douglas Congdon-Martin, Herbert N. Schiffer and Peter N. Schiffer.

Copyright © 1991 by Schiffer Publishing, Ltd.
Library of Congress Catalog Number: 90-60956.

Printed in the United States of America.
ISBN: 0-88740-320-4

Published by Schiffer Publishing, Ltd.
1469 Morstein Road
West Chester, Pennsylvania 19380
Please write for a free catalog.
This book may be purchased from the publisher.
Please include $2.00 postage.
Try your bookstore first.

We are interested in hearing from authors
with book ideas on related subjects.

American eagle weaving.
Courtesy, Foutz Trading Company.

Saddle blanket. Woven by Oliver's old sister, Old Maud. Courtesy, Private Collection.

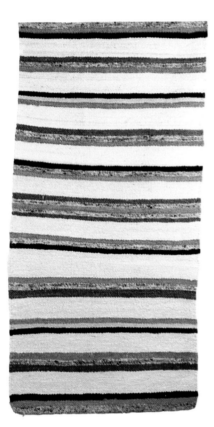

Tufted rug with brown stripes. Woven by Bessie Jones, Blanding, Utah. Courtesy, Hubbell Trading Post.

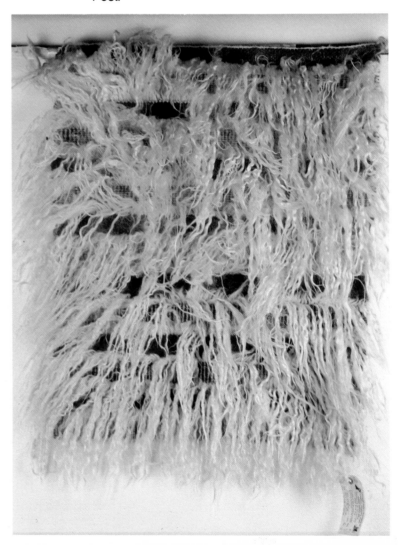

Double saddle blanket. Woven by Connie Dayzie, Cow Springs, Arizona. 30″ x 60″. Courtesy, Hubbell Trading Post.

Geometric multi-patterned four-in-one weaving. Styles from lower left clockwise: Two Grey Hills, Storm pattern, Teec Nos Pos, Ganado. Woven by Shirley Lopez. 59½" x 39½". Courtesy, Hogback Trading Post.

Round weaving. Woven, with a wheel frame as the support, by Barbara Begay. 15". Courtesy, Foutz Trading Company.

Storm pattern weaving. Woven by Angela Begaye, Ganado, Arizona. 42" x 60". Courtesy, Hubbell Trading Post.

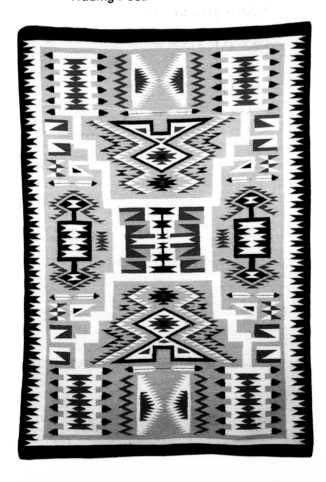

Four-in-one weaving, Two Grey Hills style. Woven by Anna Mae Tanner, 1984. 47" x 69". Courtesy, Private Collection on permanent loan to Ohio University.

Raised outline storm pattern in vegetal colors. Woven by Susie Yazzie, Chinle, Arizona. 40" x 58". Courtesy, Hubbell Trading Post.

American Flag. Woven by Cecilia Harvey, Many Farms, Arizona. 28" x 40". Courtesy, Hubbell Trading Post.

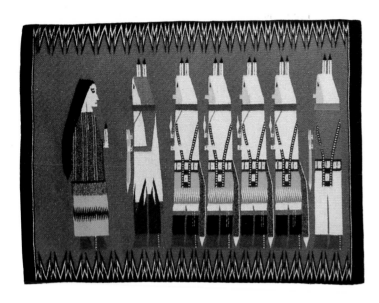

Weaving of Yei bi chei dancers in pictorial style. Woven by Della Woody. 23½" x 17". Courtesy, Kiva Indian Trading Post.

Pictorial weaving with animals. Woven by Betty Nez. 2'7" x 2'7". Courtesy, Keams Canyon Arts & Crafts.

Miniature pictorial weaving with two maidens. Woven by Betty Platero and Mary A. Begay. 7½" x 9½". Courtesy, Private Collection.

Miniature pictorial weaving with a house and six cows. 15¼" x 12½". Courtesy, Lynn Trusdell.

Pictorial weaving in a style known to some as "reservation roads" for the scene of Navajo daily life shown. Woven by Laura Nez. 42" x 28". Courtesy, Foutz Trading Company.

Corn plant tree of life with birds and the Navajo medicine basket. Courtesy, Hubbell Trading Post.

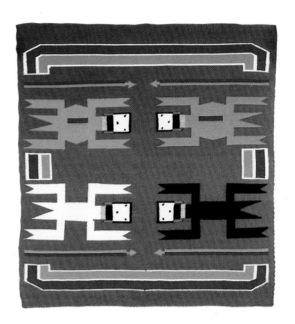

Ceremonial sandpainting design showing figures in the four sacred colors of Navajo religion: East-white, South-blue, West-yellow, North-black. Woven by Rita Gilmore, Chinle, Arizona. 32" x 35". Courtesy, Hubbell Trading Post.

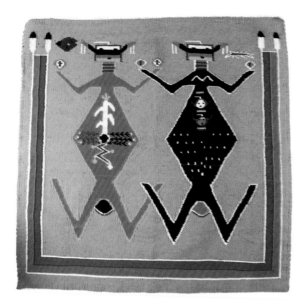

Ceremonial sandpainting weaving showing Mother Earth (blue) and Father Sky (black) within a rainbow. Inside the Mother figure are shown the four sacred plants: corn, beans, squash and tobacco. 32" x 31½". Courtesy, Turquoise Lady.

Weaving with yellow background and a fascinating design in storm pattern organization including a landscape and many animals, vehicles, and Navajo symbols. Woven by Norma Harrison. Courtesy, Private Collection.

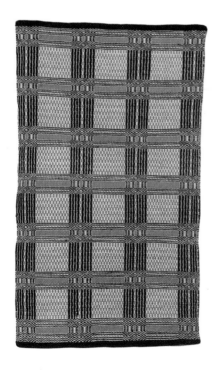

Double weave twill pattern with one side in black design and the reverse with blocked cloud pattern. Woven by Ruth Corley, 1981. 50" x 30". Courtesy, Private Collection on permanent loan to Ohio University.

POTTERY

Small pottery. Made by Alice Cling. 3¼". Courtesy, Hubbell Trading Post.

Utilitarian pottery has been made by Navajo people from abundant natural clay since they inhabited the land which is today in the states of Arizona and New Mexico. Decorations are generally sparse on the dark brown ground and the forms are regular round shapes. Recently, the pottery has been made more for sale than for their own use, and therefore the decorations have become more elaborate to appeal to the wider public.

Pot. Made by Alice Cling. 9" x 7". Courtesy, Arroyo Trading Post.

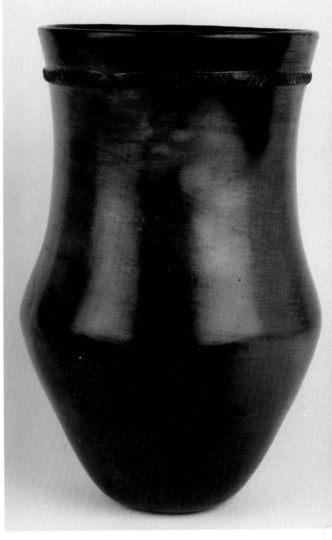

Pot with cut step pattern on the side. Made by Alice Cling. 6¾" x 4¾". Courtesy, Foutz Trading Company.

Pot. Made by Alice Cling. 15" x 10". Courtesy, Foutz Trading Company.

Pot. Made by John Whitethorn, Cow Springs, Shonto. 10" x 8". Courtesy, Foutz Trading Company.

Kachina-scratch decorated pot. Made by Faye Btso. 16¾". Courtesy, Keams Canyon Arts & Crafts.

Pot. Made by Suzie Williams. 8" x 6". Courtesy, Foutz Trading Company.

Pot with horizontal bands. Made by Louise Goodman. 12" x 10". Courtesy, Foutz Trading Company.

Two pots, one with corn ears decoration. 9". Pot with frog decoration in relief. 8". Made by Myra Tso. Courtesy, Keams Canyon Arts & Crafts.

Bowl with scratch decoration. Made by Virginia Shortman. 4″ x 8½″. Courtesy, Kiva Indian Trading Post.

Pottery bowl with scratch decoration. Made by John Whiterock, 1982. Courtesy, Turquoise Lady.

Pot with incised geometric design. Made by Lorraine Williams, Cortez, N.M. 12″ x 17″ x 17″. Courtesy, Foutz Trading Company.

Pot and detail of decoration. Made by Lorraine Williams, Cortez, N.M. 13″ x 18″ x 18″. Courtesy, Foutz Trading Company.

Three pots with side handles. Made by R.B. Left to right: 7″ x 6″, 7″ x 5½″, 6″ x 6″. Courtesy, Shiprock Trading Company.

Pot with two braided handles. Made by Suzie Williams. 9″ x 8½″. Courtesy, Shiprock Trading Company.

Lizard decoration on round pot. 10″. Marriage jar pottery vessel with two spouts. 9¼″. Made by Myra Tso. Courtesy, Keams Canyon Arts & Crafts.

Water pot with ring neck and two loops for a long shoulder strap. Made by Bene M. 9″. Courtesy, Kiva Indian Trading Post.

Pot with two side handles. Made by Rose Williams. 6½″ x 7″. Courtesy, Foutz Trading Company.

Mug with clay band around neck and twisted handle. Made by Louise Goodman. 4¼" x 5". Courtesy, Foutz Trading Company.

Coffee pot and two cups with handles. 6½" x 5½". Courtesy, Shiprock Trading Company.

Tall pot with pottery produce in three outside pockets. Made by Lorraine Williams, Cortez, N.M. 12½" x 9". Courtesy, Foutz Trading Company.

Three pots with relief decoration. Made by J Wms. Smallest pot, 5" x 7". Pot with corn, 7" x 7". Pot with eagle, 7" x 7". Courtesy, Shiprock Trading Company.

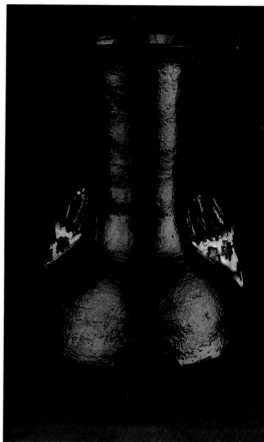

Corn pot with tall neck and applied pockets. Made by Elizabeth Many-goats. 12½" x 8". Courtesy, Kiva Indian Trading Post.

Three clay pipe bowls. Made by J Wms. 1½″ x 3½″. Courtesy, Shiprock Trading Company.

Clay pipe bowl. Made by Rose Williams. 1⅞″ x 3½″. Courtesy, Foutz Trading Company.

Double neck marriage vase. Made by Elsie Black Whitethorn. 9″ x 6½″. Courtesy, Foutz Trading Company.

Double neck wedding vase with relief decoration of a pueblo village. Made by Elsie Black. 9″ x 5½″. Courtesy, Foutz Trading Company.

Double neck wedding vase. Made by Alice Manygoats, 1981, Window Rock, Arizona. Courtesy, Turquoise Lady.

Two double neck wedding vases. Short vase, 6″ x 5″ x 5″, with pig face made by Lorraine Bartlett. Tall vase, 8″ x 6″ x 5″, with turtle made by Betty Manygoats. Courtesy, Foutz Trading Company.

Clay fetish of a little bear. Made by Williams. 1⅞" x 7¾". Courtesy, Foutz Trading Company.

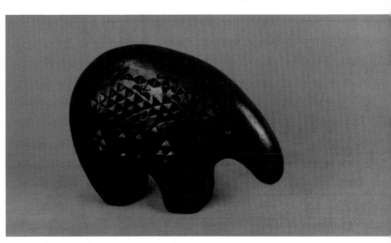

Clay black bear figure decorated with arrows and triangles. Made by Calvin Yazzie. 4¾" x 6¾". Courtesy, Foutz Trading Company.

Two clay pig-shaped coin banks. Made by John Whitethorn. 8" x 7" x 9" and 4" x 4" x 4". Courtesy, Foutz Trading Company.

Clay chicken pot fetish with brown feather design. Made by Louise Goodman. 3⅜" x 8¼". Courtesy, Foutz Trading Company.

Two coin banks, one a horse. 5" x 9" x 5". The other a pig. 4" x 7" x 4". Courtesy, Kiva Indian Trading Post.

BASKETRY

The Navajo tradition of basket making has passed its useful phase and entered into a status for ceremonial uses almost exclusively. Since the time needed to gather, prepare and weave the natural grasses is so excessive in relation to the availability of industrially-made utilitarian vessels, basketmaking as a craft is dying out. From about 1900, a tabu on basket-making by Navajo weavers led them to have their neighbors to the north, the Paiutes and Utes, weave baskets for them. For Navajo ceremonies such as blessings and weddings, flat round baskets are still made with coiled yucca in black and red analin-dyed star designs. An uncolored opening (shipapu) in the colored design extends from the center to the last coil at the outer edge, and this opening points to the east. These same patterns also are made in limited numbers for sale to tourists.

Basket, five white points, two rings. 1½″ x 10″. Courtesy, Foutz Trading Company.

Basket, five white points, three rings. 2½″ x 12″. Courtesy, Foutz Trading Company.

Basket, four white points, three rings. 2¾″ x 14″. Courtesy, Foutz Trading Company.

Basket, six white points, three rings. 2½″ x 11″. Courtesy, Foutz Trading Company.

Basket, seven white points, three rings. 2″ x 12″. Courtesy, Foutz Trading Company.

Basket, six white points, two rings. 1¾″ x 10½″. Courtesy, Foutz Trading Company.

Basket, eight white points, two rings. 2″ x 13½″. Courtesy, Foutz Trading Company.

Basket, six white points, three rings. 18″. Courtesy, Keams Canyon Arts & Crafts.

Old basket showing tightly coiled work, the design is only very faint on the worn surface. 2″ x 11½″. Courtesy, Foutz Trading Company.

JEWELRY

Turquoise has been dug from deposits in Northern New Mexico by Pueblo peoples since before the Navajo entered the region. It was from them that the Navajo learned to work turquoise and use it as an ornament as beads.

For the last hundred years, silversmithing has grown to become an important art form among the Navajo. Influenced by Spanish and Mexican silver traditions, and encouraging traders on the reservation, the styles of silverwork have evolved significantly. Today, Navajo jewelers create new styles as well as perpetuate the older types. Hand work is highly regarded, while some makers use machines to some extent. New materials such as foreign gemstones and gold and European styling continue to influence the modern work.

Recently, beadwork, inspired by Plains Indian traditions, has been made by young Navajo girls and been met with considerable success in competitions and sale to outside visitors.

Machine-made silver and turquoise bracelet. Courtesy, Beebe Hopper.

Concho belt, turquoise and silver earrings, lavulite and silver earrings, and silver bracelet with inlaid coral and turquoise. Courtesy, Hogback Trading Post.

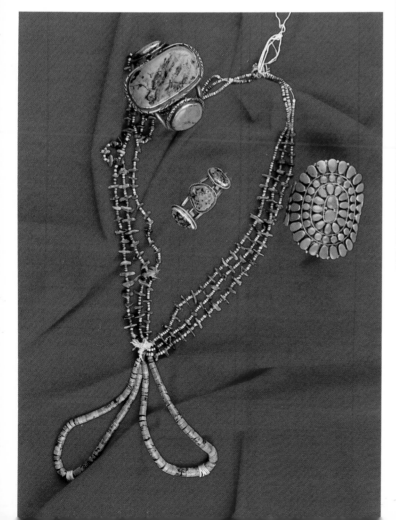

Traditional styled turquoise jewelry; turquoise and shell necklace with jocla, bracelet with three turquoise stones, bracelet with cluster by J/W, smaller bracelet with three stones by H.C. Harvey, Sr. Courtesy, Hogback Trading Post.

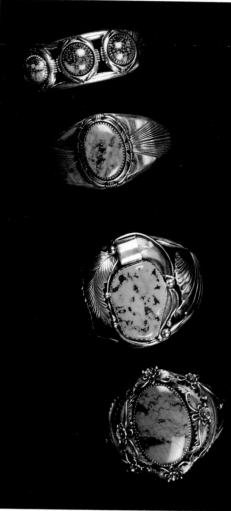

Silver necklace in the squash blossom style with bear claws and turquoise. Courtesy, Turquoise Lady.

Old style jewelry, two belts, necklace. Made by Perry Shorty, Ganado, 1990. Courtesy, Hubbell Trading Post.

Bracelets with stone inlay. From top to bottom: green turquoise 3-stone bracelet and bracelet with single oval stone, made by Jimmy Secatero; turquoise with bear claw made by A.L.; large oval made by P. Johnson. Courtesy, Palms Trading Company.

Belt buckles. Silver by S.Y. Green stone by Tommy Singer. Cluster turquoise by A. Yazzie. Beaded design by L.C. Courtesy, Palms Trading Company.

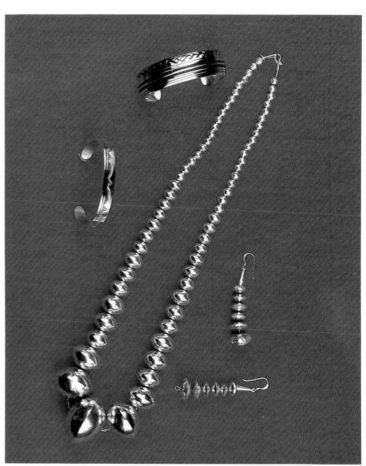

Group including a silver bead necklace, silver buckle, and Bolo set. All made by Howard Nelson, 1990. An inlaid stone buckle made by H. Smith. Courtesy, McGee's Beyond Indian Tradition Gallery.

All-silver jewelry including a graduated bead necklace and matching earrings, bracelet by Rose A. Chee, bracelet with gold by Tommy Singer. Courtesy, Hogback Trading Post.

Green turquoise set including a squash blossom necklace, three bracelets, and two rings. This special turquoise was dug at the Tiffany mine at Cerillos, N.M. Courtesy, Beebe Hopper.

Contemporary turquoise-set silver jewelry, including a style of squash blossom necklace, six bracelets, and three pins. Made by Perry Shorty, Ganado, 1990. Resting on a brilliant Wide Ruins area style weaving. Courtesy, Hubbell Trading Post.

Five-piece set of silver jewelry with coral including a ring, cuff bracelet, earrings, and link necklace. Made by B. Piaso, Jr., 1990. Courtesy, Palms Trading Company.

Three bolo, the clasps of silver, each set with a different colored turquoise. Courtesy, Palms Trading Company.

Three-piece turquoise and silver set including bracelet, ring, and link necklace with pendant. Made by Peterson Johnson, 1990. Courtesy, Palms Trading Company.

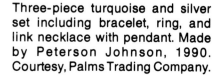

Necklace of silver with feather and bear fetish design and cuff bracelet set with turquoise. Made by B. Begay. Courtesy, Turquoise Lady.

Five silver bracelets. Bracelet with horse and man made by Tommy Singer. Other bracelets with finely wrought leaves and with geometric designs made by Peterson Johnson, 1990. Courtesy, Palms Trading Company.

Silver pendant and ring set with branch coral. Made by Loren Begay. Courtesy, Beebe Hopper.

Two sterling silver cuff bracelets. Lower bracelet with Kachina mask design by S.E. Nez. Top bracelet showing a woman spinning and a man sleeping by B & T, 1990. Courtesy, McGee's Beyond Indian Tradition Gallery.

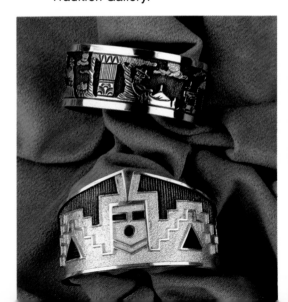

Assorted silver button covers, a new form of jewelry, 1990. Courtesy, Palms Trading Company.

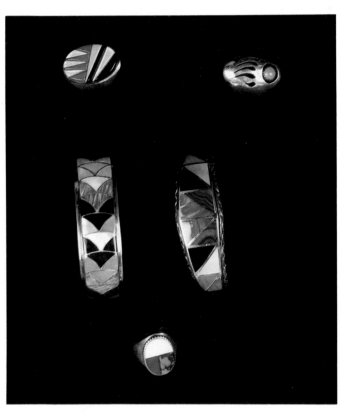

Rings and bracelets in modern designs of colorful stone inlay. Made by Orlinda Natewa. Courtesy, Palms Trading Company.

Five stone inlay silver bracelet. Courtesy, Turquoise Lady.

Group of earrings of various designs in silver and set with lavulite and turquoise. Courtesy, Palms Trading Company.

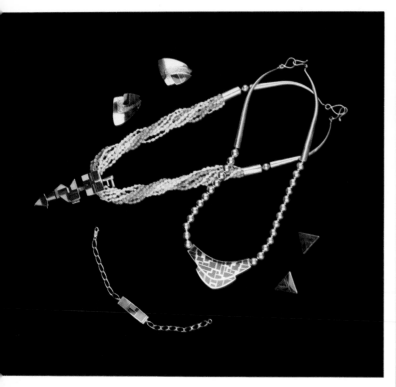

Necklace with silver beads and enameled panel, coral and biwa pearl bead necklace with inlaid pendant, malachite and silver triangular earrings, and link silver bracelet with green turquoise and lapis inlay, silver loop earrings with malachite and lavulite inlay. All by Ray Tracey, 1990. Courtesy, Hubbell Trading Post.

Bracelet and two rings of gold with turquoise, coral, lapis, opal, and onyx. Necklace of coral beads with lapis, turquoise and gold. All made by Bitsui & Russell. Courtesy, Hubbell Trading Post.

Bracelet of gold with coral, turquoise, opal, lapis and lavulite inlay. Ring and earrings of gold with stone inlay. Pendant of silver with assorted stone inlay. Bracelet with green turquoise and assorted stone inlay. All made by Raymond Yazzie. Courtesy, Hubbell Trading Post.

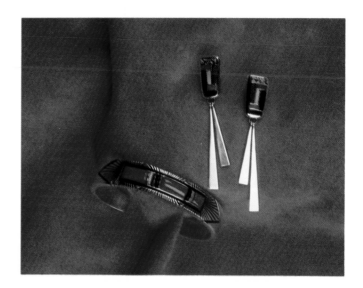

Bracelet of gold with coral inlay. Made by Raymond Yazzie. Pair of silver dangle earrings with stone inlay. Courtesy, Hubbell Trading Post.

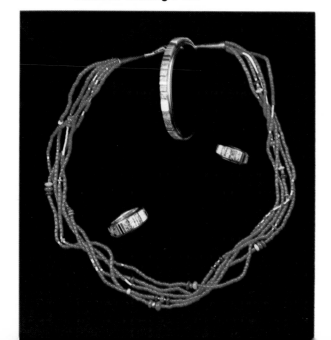

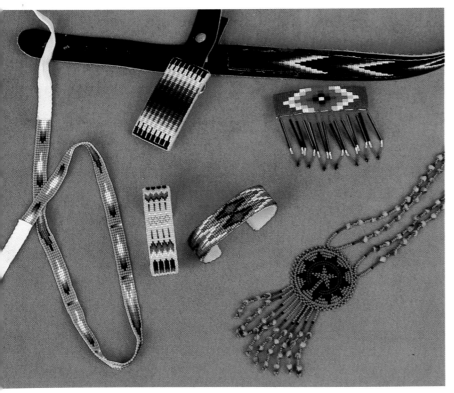

Awarded beadwork jewelry, a matching set for the Queen of a fair. Necklace and bolo tie, headband, belt, bracelet, and belt buckle. Courtesy, Turquoise Lady.

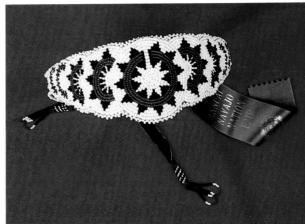

Navajo beadwork decorating a belt, buckle, headband, two bracelets, hair clip and necklace. Courtesy, Arroyo Trading Post.

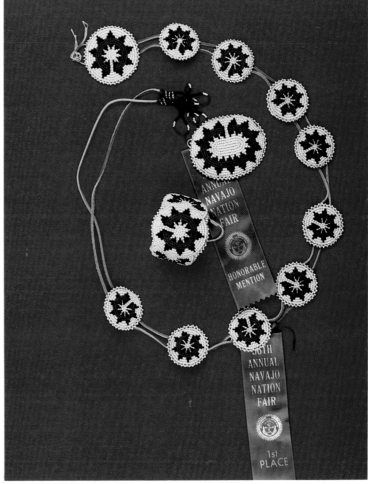

DOLLS

There are a variety of dolls made by Navajo craftsmen, all intended for sale to the outside world. Stuffed cloth, clay and cardboard are materials popularly transformed into dolls. Others are carved of wood and decorated with cloth, beads, fur, leather, feathers, etc. to replicate clothing and costumes of their everyday and ceremonial lives. From their Hopi and Zuni neighbors, whose cultures include kachinas, the Navajos have borrowed the idea of making ornamental figures. But since they are not native to the Navajo religion, even when they portray interpretations of the Hopi or Zuni kachinas, these are not rightly called kachinas; they are referred to as dolls.

Eagle dance doll. Carved by A. McB. 10¾". Courtesy, Palms Trading Company.

Carved doll, wood, fur, wool. Courtesy, Palms Trading Company.

Carved doll, wooden with cloth, beads, and feathers. 12" x 3" x 3". Courtesy, Shiprock Trading Company.

Black ogre doll, wood, wool, feathers, and leather. Carved by Harvey Laneman, 1975, Mexican Water, Arizona. 10½" x 4" x 4". Courtesy, Shiprock Trading Company.

Carved doll, wood, cloth, leather and feathers. 10½" x 2½" x 2½". Courtesy, Shiprock Trading Company.

Hoop Dancer doll. Carved by Raymond Parkett. 18¾". Courtesy, Palms Trading Company.

Clown doll. Carved by VA. 12½". Courtesy, Palms Trading Company.

Squash doll. Carved by Raymond Parkett. 15". Courtesy, Palms Trading Company.

Eagle Dancer doll. 18¼". Carved by N. Smith. Courtesy, Palms Trading Company.

Spear Dancer doll. 17½". Courtesy, Palms Trading Company.

Sunface doll. Carved by Raymond Parkett. 15¾". Courtesy, Palms Trading Company.

Carved doll. 12½". Courtesy, Palms Trading Company.

Chasing Star doll. Carved by S.A. 16". Courtesy, Palms Trading Company.

Black Bear Dance doll. Carved by L. McB. 18¾". Courtesy, Palms Trading Company.

Buffalo doll. Carved by Nelson. 18¾". Courtesy, Palms Trading Company.

Mudhead doll and child. Carved by P.S. Foster. 25½". Courtesy, Palms Trading Company.

Grey Wolf doll. Carved by Double Tameclah. 16". Courtesy, Palms Trading Company.

Toho Mountain Lion doll. 14¾". Courtesy, Palms Trading Company.

Three clowns doll. Carved by Foster. 31½". Courtesy, Palms Trading Company.

Ogre doll. Carved by A. Smith. 18½". Courtesy, Palms Trading Company.

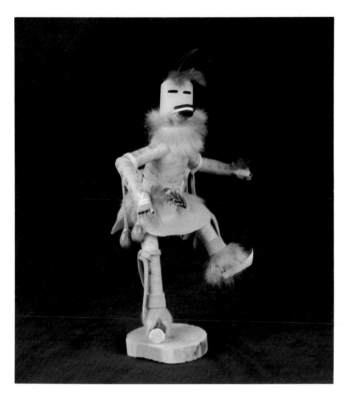

Antelope doll. Carved by Largo. 10″. Courtesy, Palms Trading Company.

Blue Sand Snake doll. Carved by Chava. 10″. Courtesy, Palms Trading Company.

Chasing Star doll. Made by L.C. 15¼″. Courtesy, Palms Trading Company.

Mocking bird doll. Carved by Smith. 11″. Courtesy, Palms Trading Company.

Koyemsi Mudhead clown doll. Carved by N. Smith. Courtesy, Palms Trading Company.

Mudhead doll. Made by Raymond Parkett. 16½". Courtesy, Palms Trading Company.

Matya hand doll. 16". Courtesy, Palms Trading Company.

Owl doll. Made by Raymond Parkett. 15½". Courtesy, Palms Trading Company.

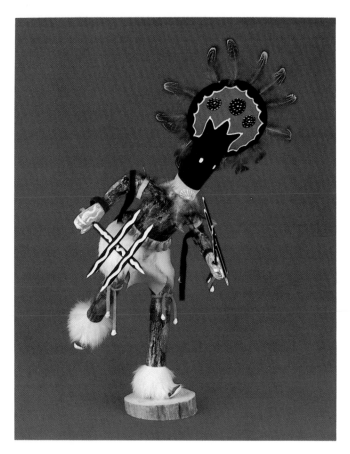

Clown Dancer doll. Made by A. McB. 18¾". Courtesy, Palms Trading Company.

Wupamo or Long Billed doll. Made by N. Joe. 15¼". Courtesy, Palms Trading Company.

Owl doll. 18½". Courtesy, Palms Trading Company.

White wolf doll. Made by Sarah Laneman. 18". Courtesy, Palms Trading Company.

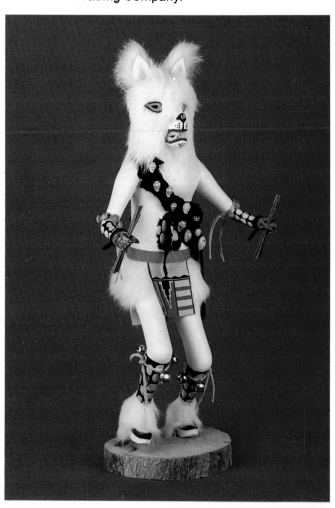

Watermelon Clown doll. Made by S. Nelson. 17¼". Courtesy, Palms Trading Company.

White buffalo doll. 14½". Courtesy, Palms Trading Company.

Hemis Dancer doll. Made by N. Joe. 19". Courtesy, Palms Trading Company.

Grey Wolf doll. Made by I. McB. 19¼". Courtesy, Palms Trading Company.

Stuffed doll grinding flour with child in cradle board. Courtesy, Palms Trading Company.

Stuffed doll with three children, all cloth. 6″ x 12″. Courtesy, Palms Trading Company.

Two stuffed dolls with infants. 2″ x 4″. Courtesy, Palms Trading Company.

Two stuffed dolls, large woman on horse with seven children, small woman on horse with infant. Courtesy, Palms Trading Company.

Stuffed woman on horse with seven children. 12″ x 10″ x 4″. Courtesy, Palms Trading Company.

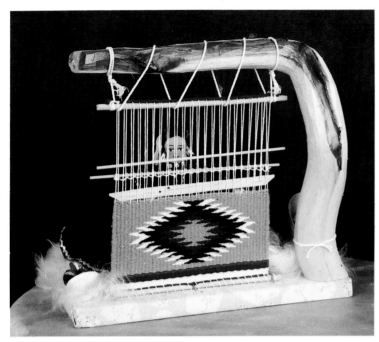

Front and back view, doll with infant at the weaving loom. Made by Della Begay. 12" x 12" x 9". Courtesy, Hogback Trading Post.

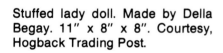

Stuffed man and woman dolls. Courtesy, Schiffer Publishing Collection.

Two large stuffed dolls of a girl and a boy. 32". Courtesy, The Congdon-Martin Collection.

Stuffed lady doll. Made by Della Begay. 11" x 8" x 8". Courtesy, Hogback Trading Post.

Mud Toy depicting a Fire Dance. Made by Lillian Brown. 7" x 18" x 18". Courtesy, Arroyo Trading Post.

Mud toy depicting a Squaw Dance. Made by Lillian Brown. 12" x 12". Courtesy, Arroyo Trading Post.

Mud toy depicting a Sweat lodge and purification ceremony. Made by Lillian Brown. 7" x 16" x 16". Courtesy, Arroyo Trading Post.

Mud toy depicting a healing ceremony with sandpainting. Made by Lillian Brown. 7" x 16" x 16". Courtesy, Arroyo Trading Post.

Mud and wood toys: woman and baby on horse, 5" x 5" x 2"; Buffalo, 4" x 4" x 2"; Cart, 6" x 11" x 5"; man and child, 6" x 5" x 2"; child on bull, 4" x 4" x 2". Made by Elsie and Sam Benally. Courtesy, Judy and Jack Beasley.

Cardboard art. Sheep 24" x 27". Calf 24" x 19". Made by Mamie Deschittie. Courtesy, Judy and Jack Beasley.

Cardboard art. Purple donkey with yellow bird, 24" x 23". Tan horse with red bird, 19" x 2". Made by Mamie Deschittie. Courtesy, Judy and Jack Beasley.

Cardboard art, calf with bird, 13" x 15", and horse with rider, 29" x 27". Made by Mamie Deschillie. Courtesy, Judy and Jack Beasley.

SANDPAINTING

The sandpainting art form has evolved gradually from religious designs executed on the earth floors of Navajo homes in loose, naturally colored sands. Since the 1960s, commercial sandpaintings have become an art form of natural and synthetically dyed sand glued to a chipboard support. The designs may reflect their religious origins, or they may be entirely creative patterns.

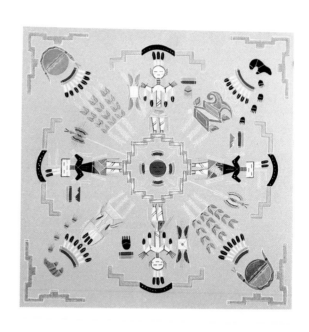

Sandpainting, Home of the Bear. Made by Thomas and Cora Bryant. 18" x 18". Courtesy, Arroyo Trading Post.

Sandpainting, black background. 24" x 24". Courtesy, Arroyo Trading Post.

Sandpainting with four designs: buffalo people, rainbow people, Home of the Bear & Snake, Coyote stealing fire. Made by Thomas and Cora Bryant. 18" x 18". Courtesy, Arroyo Trading Post.

Sandpainting, Coyote Stealing Fire. Made by Thomas and Cora Bryant. 18″ x 18″. Courtesy, Arroyo Trading Post.

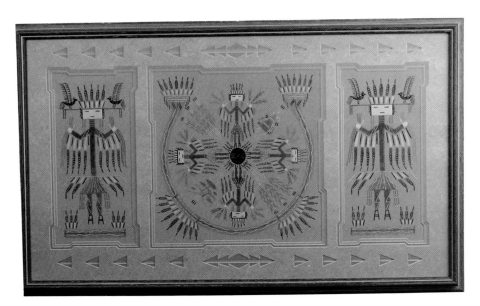

Sandpainting, 3 panels: female yei, whirling logs, female yei. Made by Benally, Jr. 15½″ x 9½″. Courtesy, McGee's Beyond Indian Tradition Gallery.

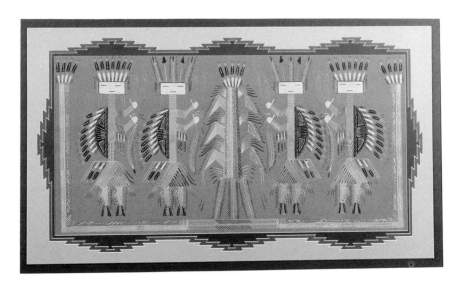

Sandpainting, four yei figures and corn plant. Courtesy, Arroyo Trading Post.

Sandpainting, central design with feathers. 12" x 12". Courtesy, Arroyo Trading Post.

Sandpainting, broken pot and petroglyphs by Jerald Sherman. Courtesy, Arroyo Trading Post.

Sandpainting, figure in blanket, pueblo, and pottery bowl. Made by Jerald Sherman. Courtesy, Arroyo Trading Post.

Sandpainting, Kachina, pottery bowl and bear. Made by Keith Silversmith. 16" x 16". Courtesy, Arroyo Trading Post.

Sandpainting, Kachina dancer. Made by Jerald Sherman. Matted with nickle concha. 24" x 18". Courtesy, Arroyo Trading Post.

Still-life of Navajo art objects by Jerald Sherman, matted with prayer stick. 18" x 24". Courtesy, Arroyo Trading Post.

Sandpainting, End of the Trail. Made by Janice Charles. 18½" x 18½". Courtesy, Foutz Trading Company.

PAINTING

From ancient pictographs on rock walls to pencils, paper and paints, Navajo artists have recorded their lives through linear art. As new materials have been introduced to them, painters have explored their manipulation to reflect their own creative expressions. Watercolor, oil and acrylic paints all are used today. The paintings usually depict the local landscape and everyday people, and therefore have been popular among visitors to the Southwest.

Painting of three people riding a horse, with ceremonial symbols. Painted by Harrison Begay. 18″ x 17″. Courtesy, Private Collection.

Painting of a squaw and child. Painted by Ts. Yazzie. 13″ x 12″. Courtesy, Private Collection.

Painting of men playing a card game in the shade of a summer shelter. Painted by Charley Yazzie. 18″ x 27″. Courtesy, Private Collection.

Painting of a costumed dancer. Painted by Charley Yazzie. 22″ x 14″. Courtesy, Private Collection.

Painting of a young boy with a sling shot. Painted by Charley Yazzie. 19″ x 11″. Courtesy, Private Collection.

Painting of a silversmith. Painted by Charley Yazzie. 22″ x 14″. Courtesy, Private Collection.

Painting of a young girl running. Painted by Ts. Yazzie. 16″ x 12″. Courtesy, Private Collection.

Painting of men engaged in a tug of war with prize watermelons awaiting the victors. Painted by Robert Chee (1937-1971) circa 1965. 17" x 38". Courtesy, Private Collection.

Bust painting of a young boy with ceremonial decorations. Painted by Robert Chee circa 1965. 18" x 13". Courtesy, Private Collection.

Painting of a running horse. Painted by Robert Chee circa 1965. 15" x 10". Courtesy, Private Collection.

Painting of two men dancing around a medicine basket. Painted by Robert Chee circa 1965. 14" x 20". Courtesy, Private Collection.

Tempera on paper, head portrait of a woman. Painted by W. Charley, 1989. 6½″ x 6½″. Courtesy, Shiprock Trading Company.

Tempera on paper, portrait. Painted by W. Charley, 1988. 11″ x 8″. Courtesy, Shiprock Trading Company.

Oil on canvas, head portrait of an aged man. Painted by Tony M. Sandoval circa 1970. 16″ x 12″. Courtesy, Shiprock Trading Company.

Oil on canvas, head portrait of an aged man with wide brimmed hat. Painted by Tony M. Sandoval, 1973. 18″ x 14″. Courtesy, Shiprock Trading Company.

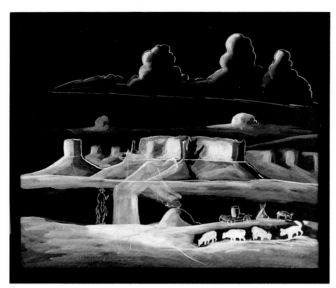

Chalk drawing of Southwest landscape. Made by Tsinajinnie. 16″ x 19″. Courtesy, Private Collection.

Watercolor painting of Southwest landscape. Painted by Tony Begay. 11″ x 15″. Courtesy, Private Collection.

Painting of two pottery bowls with turquoise beads. Painted by Jimmy Yellowhair. 20″ x 16″. Courtesy, Keams Canyon Arts & Crafts.

Winter landscape with man leading horse. Painted with acrylics by Bobby Johnson. Courtesy, Hogback Trading Company.

Acrylic. Painted by Bobby Johnson. 24" x 12". Courtesy, Private Collection of Helen and Vince Ferrari.

Landscape with pot shards, acrylics on masonite, with sand texture. Painted by Bobby Johnson. 24" x 32". Courtesy, Private Collection of Helen and Vince Ferrari.

Painting of ceremonial dancers. By
Robert Yellowhair. 24″ x 48″.
Courtesy, Private Collection.

Ceremonial clown. Painted by
Robert Yellowhair, 1970. 24″ x 12″.
Courtesy, Private Collection.

Painting in acrylic on canvas of
ceremonial dancer with large
pottery bowl. Painted by N. Naha.
19″ x 16″. Courtesy, Keams Canyon
Arts & Crafts.

WOOD CARVING

A recently-developed craft form, wood carving is taking on the naive, folk art aspects of creativity among the Navajo. Whereas dolls are made to accurately represent dancers, for example, wood carvings express a less defined image, merely the idea of the object they represent. Therefore, in almost caricatural simplicity, wood carvings provoke humor and fantasy. They have proven to be popular tourist items because of their light-hearted personalities.

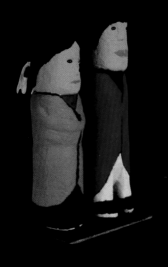

Wood carvings of two women wrapped in blankets and a rabbit. Carved by J. Antonio. Tall woman 17" x 4½", small woman 8" x 2", rabbit 6½" x 3" x 2". Courtesy, Judy and Jack Beasley.

Wood carving of a man and woman standing wrapped in blankets. Carved by Alonso Herbert, 1990. 11" x 6" x 4". Courtesy, Judy and Jack Beasley.

Wood carving of a duck and chick. Carved by Edith John. 10" x 16" x 7". Courtesy, Judy and Jack Beasley.

Wood carvings of a man, 11" x 4", and woman, 12" x 5", in traditional Navajo dress. Carved by Johnson Antonio. Courtesy, Judy and Jack Beasley.

Wood carving of an owl. Carved by Edith John. 22". Courtesy, Judy and Jack Beasley.

Cars. Made by Ronald Malone. Smaller 3" x 5" x 3"; larger 4" x 11" x 4". Courtesy, Judy and Jack Beasley.

Wood and clay Christmas figures. Left to right: Santa on giraffe 5" x 4" x 2" made by Mamie Deschillie; Santa on horse 5" x 5" x 2" made by Mamie Deschillie; small Santa ornament 2½" x 1" made by Elsie Benally; Santa on chicken 10" x 11" x 1". Made by Delbert Buck. Courtesy, Judy and Jack Beasley.

Rabbit. Made by Lula Yazzie. 11½" x 4" x 7". Courtesy, Judy and Jack Beasley.

Rooster Riders of wood. Carved by Delbert Buck. Left: 10" x 17" x 6". Right: 16" x 15" x 5". Courtesy, Judy and Jack Beasley.

Skunk carvings. Carved by Wilford and Lula Yazzie. Courtesy, Judy and Jack Beasley.

Man on horse, wood carving. Carved by Wilford Yazzie. 26" x 22" x 6". Courtesy, Judy and Jack Beasley.

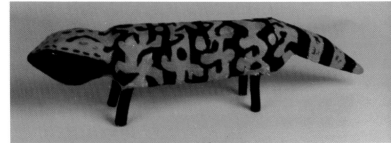

Gila monster, wood. Carved by Lula Herbert. 20" long. Courtesy, Judy and Jack Beasley.

Geese wood carvings. Carved by Wilford Yazzie. Left: 22" x 13" x 8". Right: 27" x 18" x 9". Courtesy, Judy and Jack Beasley.

Five wooden dolls. Carved by Wilford Yazzie. Left to right: 14" x 4"; 12" x 4"; center 16½" x 5"; tall 23" x 7"; 14" x 4½". Courtesy, Judy and Jack Beasley.

Wood carving of a silversmith and his tools. Carved by Jack Tsosie. 7" x 11" x 7". Courtesy, Private Collection.

Wooden dancer figure carved by
Robin Willeto, 1990. 19″ x 8″ x 3″.
Skunk carved by Harold Willeto,
1989. 12″ x 23″ x 5″. Courtesy,
Judy and Jack Beasley.

Wooden donkey. Carved by Wilford
Yazzie. 20″ x 26″ x 6″. Courtesy,
Judy and Jack Beasly.

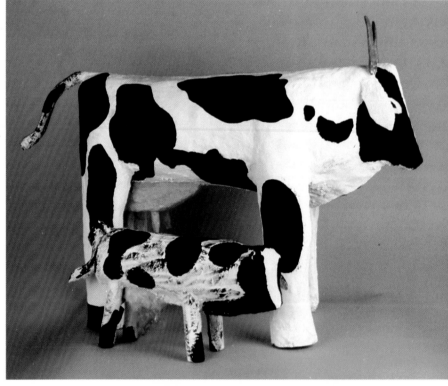

Cow and calf carved from wood.
Courtesy, Judy and Jack Beasley.

Wooden rooster. Carved by Lula
Yazzie. 23″ x 16″ x 8″. Courtesy,
Judy and Jack Beasley.

Two birds. Carved by Delbert Buck. Left: 22″ x 14″ x 8″. Right: 19″ x 12″ x 6″. Courtesy, Judy and Jack Beasley.

Wood sculpture of a standing woman holding a coiled basket tray. Carved by Bernie Tohdachenny. 24¼″. Courtesy, Foutz Trading Company.

Wood sculpture of a standing woman in blanket. Carved by C.C. Joe. 23″ x 4″ x 4″. Courtesy, Shiprock Trading Company.

Wood sculpture of a man holding a basket. Carved by Bernie Tohdachenny, Shiprock. 21″ x 6″ x 6″. Courtesy, Arroyo Trading Post.

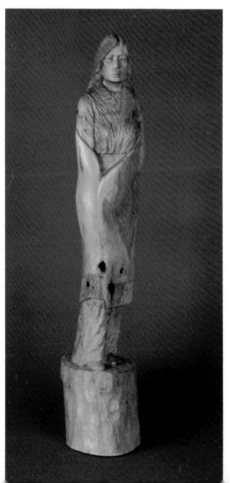

STONE SCULPTURE

Even in the midst of fantastic rock formations throughout their lands, the Navajos have not developed a long tradition of carving stone. In fact, only in the 1980s, with the encouragement of school art teachers and traders in the Shiprock area, have young carvers begun to sculpt stone into interesting forms. This new media has proven successful commercially, and continuing serious, imaginative development of the designs is anticipated.

Stone sculpture, woman. Carved by Tim Washburn, 1990. 17" x 12" x 6". Courtesy, Arroyo Trading Post.

Stone sculpture, woman seated. Carved by Orland Joe. 11" x 8" x 8". Courtesy, Shiprock Trading Company.

Stone sculpture, pipe smoker. Carved by George Benally. 12" x 8" x 6". Courtesy, Hogback Trading Post.

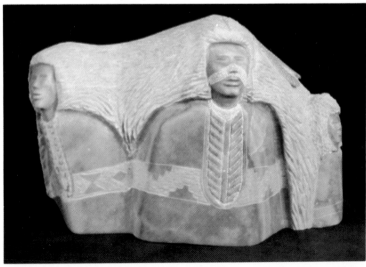

Stone sculpture. Carved by Brian Begaye. 7" x 10" x 4". Courtesy, Foutz Trading Company.

Stone sculpture of a standing figure.
Carved by Orland Joe. 14" x 5½" x
2½". Courtesy, Foutz Trading
Company.

Stone sculpture, Deer Dancer.
Carved by Franklin Foster. 25" x 8"
x 5". Courtesy, Hogback Wheeler
Collection.

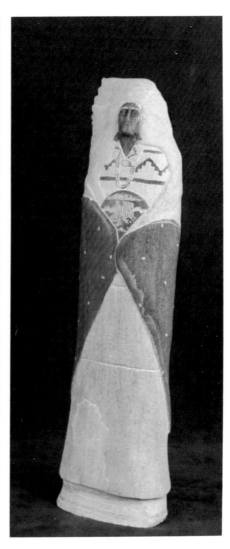

Stone sculpture, standing figure in
a blanket. Carved by Orland Joe.
16" x 4" x 2". Courtesy, Foutz
Trading Company.

Stone sculpture, four figures. Sitting
figure with blanket carved by C.C.
Joe, 6" x 3" x 3". Other figures
carved by Victor Cambridge, 1990.
Tall thin figure: 6½" x 1½" x 1½".
Shorter thin: 5" x 2½" x 2". Largest:
7½" x 4" x 4". Courtesy, Shiprock
Trading Company.

Stone sculpture. Carved by Keyionie, Herb Peterson. 16" x 13" x 9". Courtesy, Hogback Trading Post.

Stone sculpture of two figures grooming the hair of a young girl before her puberty ceremony. Carved by Greg Johnson. 16" x 7¾" x 12½". Courtesy Schiffer Publishing Collection.

Stone sculpture, front and back views. Carved by Keyionie, Herb Peterson. Courtesy, Hogback Trading Post.

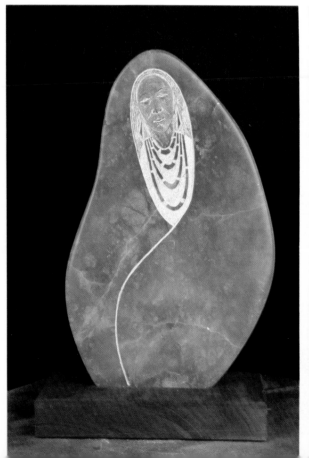

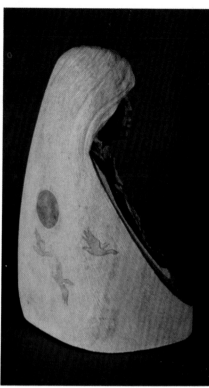

Stone sculpture, front and side views. Carved by Orland Joe. 13″ x 8″ x 9″. Courtesy, Shiprock Trading Company.

Stone sculpture of a figure seated cross-legged. Carved by Mike Toledo. 13″ x 12″ x 5″. Courtesy, Arroyo Trading Post.

Stone sculpture of a lounging figure. Carved by Mike Toledo. 15½″ x 22″ x 5″. Courtesy, Foutz Trading Company.

Stone sculpture of a woman with corn. Carved by Orland Joe. 15″ x 8″ x 5″. Courtesy, Shiprock Trading Company.

Stone sculpture, man and woman standing in blanket. Carved by Greg Johnson. 28″ x 12″ x 8″. Courtesy, Arroyo Trading Post.

Stone sculpture of seated figure with shield. Carved by Greg Johnson. 20″ x 12″ x 8″. Courtesy, Arroyo Trading Post.

Stone sculpture, head of a man with inlaid turqouise gem. Carved by Keyionie, Herb Peterson. 15″ x 11″ x 8″. Courtesy, Hogback Trading Post.

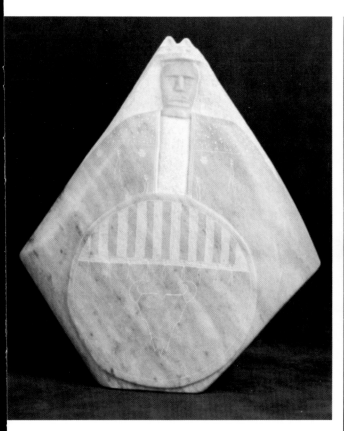

Stone sculpture of a figure with shield. Carved by David Pettigrew. 13″ x 11″ x 2″. Courtesy, Foutz Trading Company.

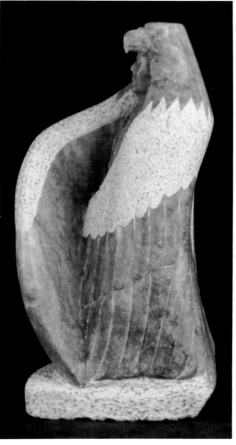

Stone sculpture of man in eagle feathers. Carved by Mike Toledo. 16″ x 8″ x 6″. Courtesy, Foutz Trading Company.

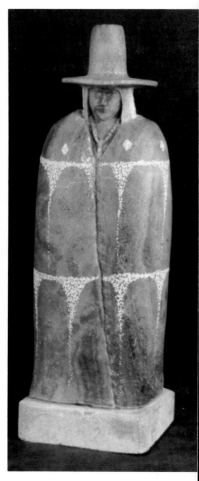

Stone sculpture, man in blanket and wide brimmed hat. Carved by Zane Barney, Kirtland. 17″ x 5″ x 4½″. Courtesy, Foutz Trading Company.

Stone sculpture of man with feathers in a blanket, front and back view. Carved by Franklin Foster. 18″ x 7″ x 7″. Courtesy, Hogback Trading Post.

Stone sculpture group of man and woman. Carved by George Benally, 1985. 18" x 16" x 6". Courtesy, Wheeler Collection, Hogback Trading Post.

Stone sculpture of aged man in blanket with walking stick, "This Land was Mine". Carved by Ron Benally. 25" x 13" x 8". Courtesy, Wheeler Collection, Hogback Trading Post.

Stone sculpture, standing woman, serpentine or soapstone. Carved by Tim Washburn. 27". Courtesy, Arroyo Trading Post.

Stone sculpture of man with stick, blanket, and shield. Carved by Brian Begaye. 13½" x 8" x 5". Courtesy, Foutz Trading Company.

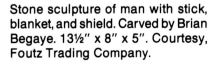

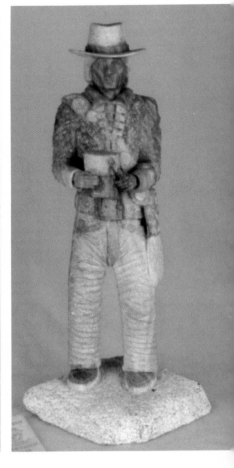

Stone sculpture of bust figure in blanket and animal headdress. Carved by Terri Pettigrew. 8½" x 9" x 4½". Courtesy, Foutz Trading Company.

Stone sculpture of a standing man. Carved by Orland Joe. 17½" x 7" x 5". Courtesy, Foutz Trading Company.

Stone sculpture of a seated man on a rock. Carved by Mike Toledo. 16" x 12" x 6". Courtesy, Hogback Trading Post.

Stone sculpture of standing man with wide-brimmed hat. Carved by Greg Johnson. Courtesy, Arroyo Trading Post.

Stone sculpture, woman's head with eagle. Carved by Marvin Toya. 5½". Courtesy, Keams Canyon Arts & Crafts.

Stone sculpture of bust figure and pueblo architecture. Carved by Gilbert Yazzie, Shiprock. 6" x 13" x 1". Courtesy, Foutz Trading Company.

FETISHES

The magical powers attributed to certain animals are transferred to believing people through images of the animals, and so the Navajo, like their Zuni neighbors, carve stone fetishes to convey these powers. Symbolic only to those who understand their powers, fetishes are also popular mementos to the uninformed.

Fetish necklace carved with many stone animals strung on eight strands of shell heishe. Carved by the Couser Brothers. Courtesy, McGee's Beyond Indian Tradition Gallery.

Bird fetish of turquoise with stone medicine bundle tied to its back. 1". Courtesy, Palms Trading Company.

Wolf fetish carved from serpentine. Courtesy, Palms Trading Company.

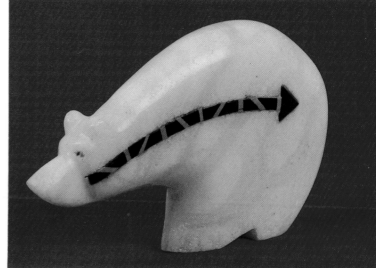

Bear fetish, Utah alabaster, turquoise and jet inlay. Carved by Livingston. Courtesy, Palms Trading Company.

Stone mountain lion fetish. Courtesy, Palms Trading Company.